WHAT'S WRONG HERE?
AT THE AMUSEMENT PARK

By

Tony Tallarico

Incorporated

ANSWERS ON LAST PAGE

The Fun Park Amusement Center is officially open for wrongdoing. You are invited to find ten things that have gone wrong on opening day.

The first stop is the Wacky Little School-house. You can come inside too and help find at least <u>ten</u> things that are wrong here.

The flume ride is almost ready to go... except for a few things that are wrong. Can you find exactly 12 things that are wrong with this picture?

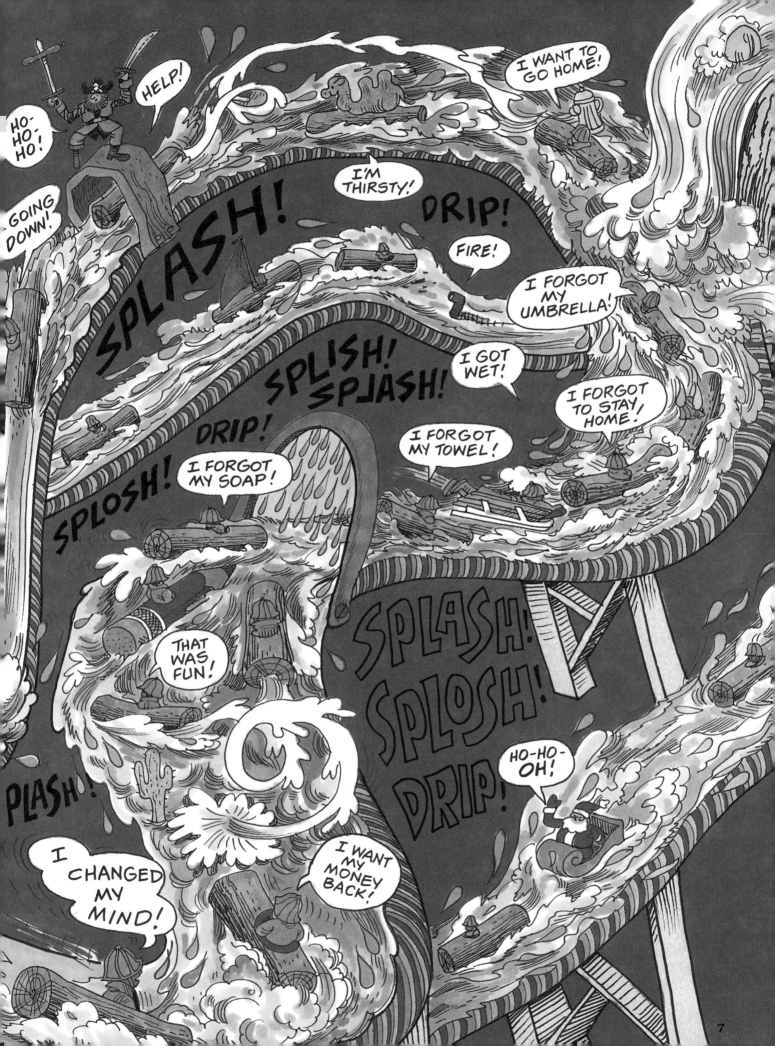

No amusement park is complete without its very own wacky circus. How many wrong things can you find here?

8

11

Welcome to the wildest roller coaster ever! Besides the thrills and chills, there are <u>ten</u> things wrong with this ride for you to find.

The amusement park is filled with fun things to do. But before you can enjoy yourself, search for and find at least 18 things that are wrong with this picture.

Have your tickets ready, please! The Toot-Toot train ride has begun. Along the way, look for and find at least <u>18</u> things that are wrong with this picture.

The last event of the day is a ride on the ferris wheel. Unfortunately, there are a number of things wrong here. How many can you find?

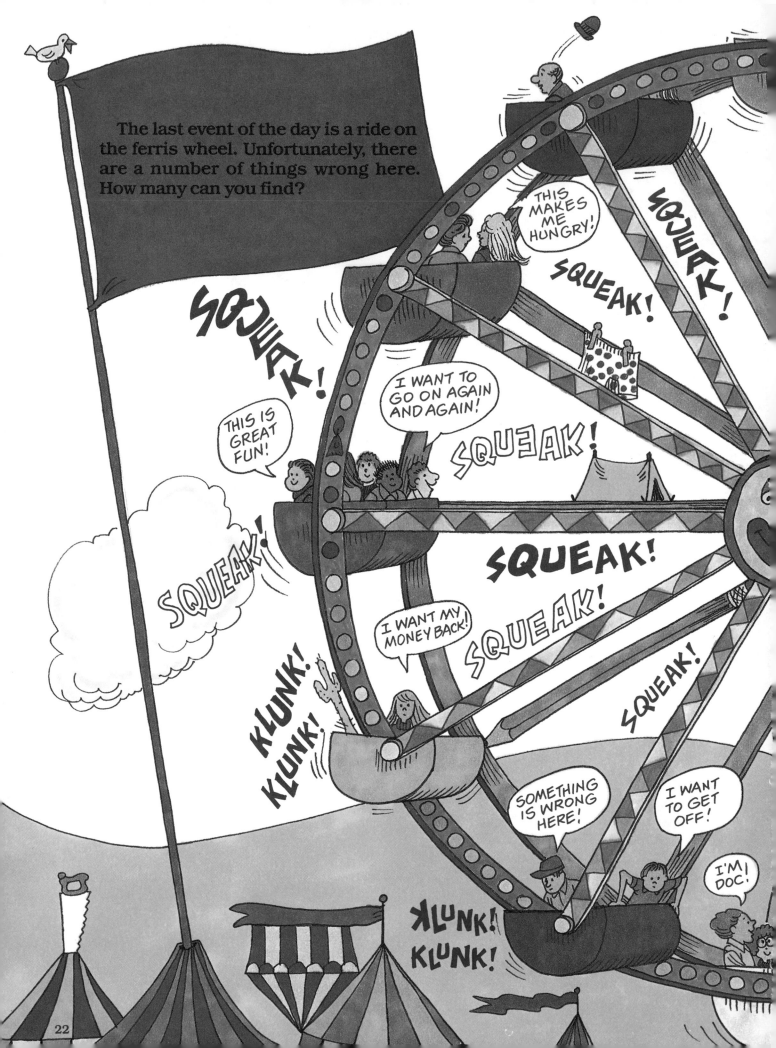

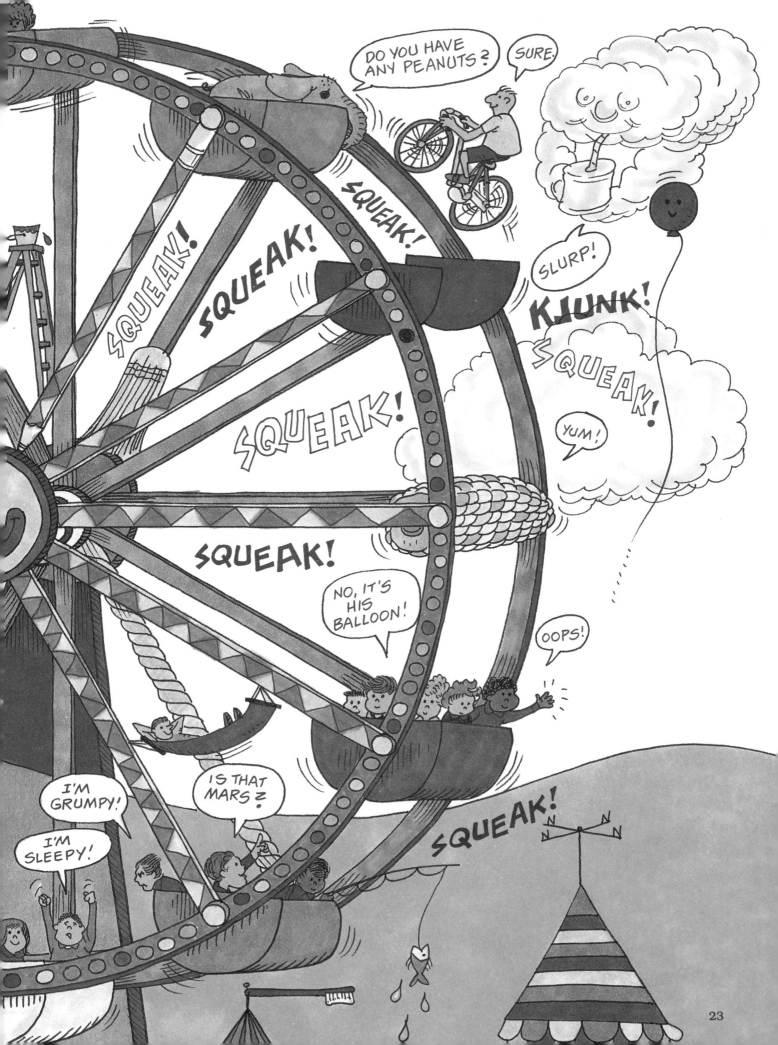